Heart Lake over looking Mt. Shasta, CA.

Our Beloved Mt. Shasta CA.
New snow covers her with a blessed blanket.

Lenticular clouds over Mt. Shasta.

Snow melted at house.
Our front yard overlooking Mt. Shasta covered
with new snow.

Stunning sunrise over Mt. Shasta from our front
yard.

Mt. Shasta from Dome on top of mountain.

Mt. Shasta after new snow.

Mt. Shasta no snow on mountain. Beautiful clouds.

Pink sky before sunset on Mt. Shasta.

Peace garden Mt. Shasta.

Mt. Shasta International Peace Garden

Pluto's cave Mt. Shasta.

Pluto's cave Mt. Shasta.

Pluto's cave Mt. Shasta, CA

Castle Lake Mt Shasta.
Very clean and pure water.

Silent Stream Hike.
Most Peaceful and Spiritual Meditation.

Silent Stream Mt Shasta.
Very Spiritual Place to hike and meditate.

Panther Meadows, Mt Shasta. This is a fantastic spiritual place.

Panther Meadows, Mt Shasta, CA.

Old Ski Bowl Trail to Mt. Shasta.

On the Old Ski Bowl Trail.

Hiking up to the mountain.

Ascension Temple, Mt Shasta CA.

Mossbrae Falls, Dunsmuir CA.

Burney Falls, majestic and beautiful hike and
State Park, has a general store, food etc.

Animals in the front yard, Mt. Shasta, CA

Pine cone mandela by dear friend, Elena